Moments Past and Present:

Selected Poems

Michael Bourgo

-2016-

ISBN-13: 978-1530063581

ISBN-10: 1530063582

Library of Congress Control Number 2016903985

Author photo: Jennie Toyokawa

Some of these poems (or earlier versions) have appeared in *Lyrical Iowa, Lucidity, Midwest Poetry Review, Encore, Pennessence, Prize Poems 2016* (PA Poetry Society) and *The Lyric*.

Create Space Independent Publishing Platform

North Charleston, South Carolina

Dedicated to

my four Js,

Leo and Maya,

and with special thanks to

my faithful readers

Contents

Pierre Paul Bourgault (1853–1904) 7
Finding the Dog (1949) 8
Moments 9
March 24, 2011 10
I Confront My Own Mortality 11
Gifts 12
November 16 13
Voyages 14
Spring Notes 15
My Last Garden 16
The Memoirists 17
For My Sister, Who Never Was 18
A Walk to School 19
Learning the World 20
The End of the Line 21
The Magic of Memory 22
A Few Thoughts at the End of March 23
Waiting for the Biopsy 24
The Mullein 25
The Spider Web 26
Evening in July 27
Applied Ethics 28
The Parts of a World 29
Yesterday 30
November 1, 2009 31
The Transports of a Friday Night 32
The Importance of Being Unimportant 33
What I Think I Know 34
Thinking about Love 35
A Farewell 36
A Reply 37
A World in Round 38
Christmas Eve 2014 39
A Long Marriage 40

Chicago 41
Moments, a Little Later 42
Snowfall at Night 43
Full Moon 44
Sunday at Bever Park 45
Today 46
The Scarlet Tanager 47
Cancer 48
The Asters 49
The Tree Outside That Window 50
For Leo Michael 51
The Moth 52
For Maya Grace 53
The Moth, Revisited 54
The Streams of Pennsylvania 55
The Quick and the Dead 56
Waiting for Maya 57
A Place to Be 58
The Lovers 59
The Snake 60
A Blessing 61
July 25, 2011 62
The End of Summer 63
Worlds 64
October 13 65
A Poem for My Latest Birthday 66
All Saints' Day 2015 67
An Ordinary Night in Boalsburg, Pennsylvania 68
November 22, 2013 69
Life Continues 70
Destinations 71

Pierre Paul Bourgault (1853–1904)

My ancestor wore himself out,
both his feet and his coronary arteries,
on the streets of Joliet, Illinois,
the cop on the beat, dead at fifty:
too many years of drunks and strikes,
of whores who worked the canal,
too many lost wives and children.

There was one photo left, a sepia ghost
posed in a high-collared tunic,
helmet in the crook of his arm.
His eyes are heavy with the weight
of four children and public order:
it's French Pete, whose nightstick
was his most effective word in English.

A northerner in search of the sun,
he had renounced the rocky pastures
and left behind the sparse hills
of dwindling Quebec. He settled
for thirty miles south of Chicago,
married Irish Margaret Meagher,
and waged war against original sin.

His children found him a stranger,
more silent each year as the letters
(which only he could read) grew scarcer,
muttering in French as his family
passed him by in their American commotions,
a man whose culture no longer fit,
who limped to the end full of thoughts
not heard out loud in years.

Finding the Dog (1949)

One fine October afternoon in Knoxville,
our middle-aged Scottie took his leave.
My mother had no love for this animal,
but to disappoint a then-absent husband
was not an admissible option,
and we passed the rest of the day
searching and calling in vain.

It was a very quiet suppertime
until someone called with news of our dog,
and herding us into coats and hats,
our mother led us on a long bus ride,
starts and stops through a darkening city,
descending at last in a distant neighborhood
a few steps from a small frame house.

She knocked, and as the door opened,
we found a black woman watching us,
old Key at her feet wagging his tail,
and after some polite conversation,
the shared knowledge of women everywhere,
smiles, thanks, and a dollar were passed,
and the dog emerged, not a bit contrite.

With the customary expertise of a parent,
she quickly conjured a taxi,
negotiating a ride with the black cabby,
the two agreeing to overlook local customs.
Making warm pile in the back seat,
mother, two small boys, and dog
were all delivered safely home,
along with questions for a lifetime.

Moments

We are counseled to live in the moment,
and so it should be. Moments do not return,
and thus, the world must be imagined
from our gathering of moments,
lest we question that it is;
much as the atoms of francium
(an element recently explained to me)
are material but so soon immaterial,
disappearing at the moment of their birth,
and then utterly gone. Forever,
just as falling leaves or rain drops,
beams of sunlight through a window,
things we can only remember—
poignantly—like those romances
of our fifteenth spring or summer,
which, naïvely, we thought eternal.

March 24, 2011

After two days of rain and snow,
of branches rustling with ice,
and winter still unrelenting,

the dog and I walked down the road
to the sounds of a thousand blackbirds.
There was a new clarity of sun,

a light falling clean and hard
through openings in the woods,
the song sparrow singing,

and a bluebird watching the field—
a step into months to come
as one time gave way to the next.

I Confront My Own Mortality

Life, it seems, is one test after another,
searching for that anomaly
that might be the final answer.
One number is too high,
and another too low,
and the cycle just rolls on,
much like those medieval theologians
who searched for the first cause,
some elusive phenomenon
that would put all questions
into their proper resting places.
I make no claims for bravery,
only a sort of resignation:
sooner or later some disorder
is going to claim the rest of my days,
whether joyfully, as in an event,
or, more likely, as life is today,
through a slow and evil process;
and meanwhile, as I wait,
it seems probable that the suspense
will surely kill me.

Gifts

Wort, noun PLANT: esp: an herbaceous plant—
usu. used in combination <toothwort>
[ME, fr. OE wyrt root, herb, plant]
   —Merriam-Webster Collegiate Dictionary

Consider all the worts,
by origin not flowers, only plants:
no roses or tulips among these,

no prize winners here,
nothing you'd find in a catalog.
They're prefixed in prose, not poetry:

motherwort, spiderwort, pennywort,
and, descending even further,
sandwort, stitchwort, and lousewort—

not one a stem that you'd cultivate—
but something that must be found
and yet bold enough to bloom,

content to be the gift
of some summer morning
along a road or near the woods.

November 16

It was a lovely, mild day,
a muddy sky but no rain,
so my dog and I were in the park.
A father and child were at the swings
as we walked through the leaves,
and the remains of the oaks, at last fallen,
taxed my imperfect knowledge—
I found pins, whites, and reds,
but one leaf remained a mystery:
and at the end of our route,
not far away, two girls were kissing—
something well out of my ken—
but why not? It's just love,
whatever the shape or form,
that feeling you know so well
when it's no longer there.

Voyages

The world is full of places
you've never seen
(and never will),
but it doesn't matter.

Your thoughts will roll on,
passing before your eyes
scenes you saw in magazines,
or imagined only from musings,
and make a landscape as real
as any you've ever seen;

and perhaps land on a Gaugin,
a picture of warmth and light
(how alive and ripe those women!),
and a scene just as tangible
as your quiet corner in Pennsylvania,
buried in the snows of February;

and soon enough you'll be home—
in time for breakfast.

Spring Notes

The world is a better place
if there are catbirds and song sparrows
to fill the day with music:
one a Mozart who knows his voice
and lays out well-ordered movements,
and the other a Charlie Parker
who's never sure of the next chorus
but ends up finding all the notes.
As the sun warms hidden places,
the stems pass through the soil
with an idea for a flower,
the intelligence of seeds at work,
and one by one, in their turn,
the trees find their leaves.
There are perhaps miracles
and then the miracles of each day—
the former we might never meet
though we waited a lifetime,
and then, the latter, available
on any day in early May,
waiting only for us to name them.

My Last Garden

I want death to find me planting my cabbages, careless of death, and still more of my unfinished garden.

—*Michel de Montaigne,* Essays (1580)

Well, sir, I have the honor of your name,
share your love for the garden,
and concur on final matters,

but I'd love to set the time,
aim for my last moments
in September or October.

I care as little as you
about this imminent departure:
it can come when it will,

but I would be most pleased
to leave some lettuce and squash
for those who survive—

good food (surely no small matter)
and a sliver of my faith—
in seeds, if nothing else.

The Memoirists

(for the Thursday group at UUFCC)

Here we sit, a circle, a gathering,
sharing our lives and our stories,
now distant but once so immediate,
and though slower in our flesh,
we hope not in the memory
of those moments that made us souls.

We write of those days when we learned,
of others when we loved or despaired,
and still others when nothing much happened,
yet hours we will call happy,
thankful of some small grace
against the inexorable odds.

And now to you, ruler of our times,
we might loose a small prayer:
give us the time and the will
to remember what was so long ago,
to shape that living into words,
and write it into eternal now.

For My Sister, Who Never Was

Small person, you lost your way
on some April day in 1943,
in that passage from water to air,
and never breathed a single moment:
my big sister who never was,
who lived only as a memory
our mother would not surrender.

I mourn that you never saw a flower,
never felt the breeze after spring rain,
when the world is new again,
or heard the robins at dawn.
We never shared games or thoughts
or walked through a season together:
you were never there to hold my hand
when I, a boy often bewildered,
would have gained from your presence,
your exploring, your older knowledge.

So I have gone on, deprived of you,
my eyes alone to know the world
and love its magic for us both;
and tonight, a misty April ten o'clock,
there is Venus, a star, and the moon,
a heavenly trio in the spring sky—
for you, me, and our mother.

A Walk to School

(for my brother)

At seven, I assumed responsibility,
marching you each morning to the church
where you went to nursery school,
a privilege I had been denied.

You were a considerable being,
almost my size and weight,
and early instruction had sharpened you
into a self-confident revolutionary.

One winter morning you lay down
in the new snow for a near eternity,
a round, defiant angel making
slow patterns of arms and legs.

You punctured my mission with giggles,
and neither rage nor pulling availed.
At last I gave up and turned away,
consigning you to yourself alone.

In a few steps your mitten slipped into mine,
and then we finished one of many walks
where my gravity was no match
for the wings of your laughter.

Learning the World

As a child, studying the atlas,
looking at the great world
spread across two pages,
I saw America in the center
and everything else to one side,
as was fitting and proper,
though parts of Asia and Russia
were repeated, both right and left,
which did not seem quite fair.
Top right were places I knew—
England, France, and Holland—
countries encountered in books,
understanding eased by similarities
(people who rode bicycles),
but below it was closer to enigma
as I read names that included
Morocco, Belgian Congo, and Malaysia—
but not entirely so, for I had stamps,
carefully mounted in my Scott's Album;
so I knew something of those environs:
knew of camels crossing the desert,
black men carrying boxes on their heads,
and rubber being collected from trees.
As I read further of these places
in my almanac and the *Weekly Reader,*
where cars and ice were scarce,
but apparently not the malevolence
of horrible disease and hidden beasts,
it was all a mix of fear and wonder,
of facts not easy to assimilate,
a grave threat to the quiet certainties
of a small boy in Aurora, Illinois,
attending second grade in 1952.

The End of the Line

It must have been about June 1955
when my brother and I, adventurers,
wanted to see the end of the line.
Our mother, a believer in autonomy, agreed,
and not sure of the rules for round trips,
gave me twenty cents, four nickels,
twice the one-way fare. Just in case.
We walked to the corner, waited,
and boarded the Downer Place bus
at the near corner on our side of the street—
unlike our downtown excursions—
and expectantly took our seats.
Soon we were in unknown realms,
beyond the three blocks we had explored,
passing houses we had never seen,
and though most were just houses,
there were chateaus of unexpected beauty
all across a wide expanse, ten minutes
filled with the marvels of gardens,
house numbers that passed 1500,
and newly discovered lawns and trees.
Finally, we reached the last street,
the entire horizon in front of the bus
filled with an endless corn field.
The bus stopped. The driver got out
and smoked a cigarette. He was in no hurry.
At last he climbed back in, turned us homeward,
and through sights now familiar,
we soon spotted Healy Funeral Parlor,
pulled the cord, and emerged,
proven explorers safely returned,
having witnessed the known world—
and with ten cents to give back to our mother.

The Magic of Memory

Are these lovely thoughts a memory
or just thoughts posing as one?
Memory is perhaps a traitor,
but at my age, it is a kindly one
when it brings a summer afternoon,
moments of sixty years ago:
my brother and I emerged from the movies,
blinking as we reentered that sunny day.

We headed for home but with careful haste,
lingering along shop windows and then lawns:
dutiful, no doubt, but in no hurry.
Waiting at home was trash to take out,
orders to take a bath and put on clean clothes,
but, for now, we could talk about cowboys,
our favorite baseball players,
or castles, knights, and other fancies.

To revisit a time when time meant nothing,
because there seemed so much of it,
to return briefly to a happy day
swelled by memory's careless generosity—
for such a gift, there is only gratitude:
veracity is a noble thing to be prized,
but thankfully we do not live under oath,
and sometimes verisimilitude will suffice.

A Few Thoughts at the End of March

Life goes on, and how do we choose?
We are either entitled or condemned
to a following day, the next chapter—

from wind and blowing snow
to the happy sounds of finches,
who know it's a better season;

though for us, not so simple,
we who cannot let mere climate
set the tempo of our steps,

who must worry about what we do
and measure the accounts
of what has been and may be,

though plain sense will tell us
that some days exist only
so that we can smell the spring.

Waiting for the Biopsy

How glamorous it is to think of death,
of glorious final conclusions,
but likely I will get something else:
more pills to take and more tests,
the bills to pay every month,
the dog to walk every morning,
and so I must do as the French say,
"Continuez, mon ami, continuez."
I'll wake up every morning,
drink coffee and read the paper,
wonder what shirt to wear
and what chores to do
from a list so religiously prepared,
and wander out every night,
hoping to see the stars.

The Mullein

It's a flower with grit,
ready to set its leaves
and a spike of yellow blooms

where no one else would go,
willing to keep company
with alleys and railroad tracks,

never needing an invitation,
the flower of those places
that have no flowers.

The Spider Web

One day while mowing the lawn,
I found a spider web
stretched across my path,

and stepping around
its shimmering net,
I left a patch uncut,

afraid perhaps of consequence,
that my pointless work
disturb both home and art.

Evening in July

Tonight, as the dog dragged me
down the sidewalk, past the houses,
much farther than I wanted to go,
my mind was empty of thoughts
and distant from any marvel.
I felt mired in a void of nothing,
mourned the lack of inspiration,
but at some point I looked up:
the clouds were painting
their wonder across the sky
as the dusk gave way to the dark,
and off in the west between the banks,
a crescent adorned with Venus
sent us both safely home
in the glorious comfort of discovery.

Applied Ethics

Better than ordinary is our credo:
a cardinal instead of a sparrow,
a rose before vervain,

but how we deceive ourselves!
Better that we understand
the heroism of each day;

grasp the beauty of the opened door,
a graceful word or two
uttered for some stranger

than await the grand gesture,
so eagerly wished but so rare
on sidewalks or in shopping malls;

and reward ourselves for such kindness,
for the gift of ourselves,
by doing it again tomorrow.

The Parts of a World

The parts of a world
are not easy to assemble.
How wide the circle is,
starting with those you love
and the stars of September,
all the things you can see
from your careful perch,
stretching to all the sights
you must make yourself know,
distant scenes far removed
from the comforts of your chair
or the bluebirds and goldenrod:
tales of courage and suffering
you can scarcely conceive;
from exile, hunger, and pain
to passages on fragile boats;
and without this knowledge,
it is a world incomplete,
and one where you must not,
for even one quiet moment,
allow yourself to live.

Yesterday

Though yesterday is now an event,
yesterday it wasn't yet
as we stepped from moment to moment,
crossed the water stone by stone,
followed that glorious chain of points,
a network of stars and lights.
It was something and then something new;
there was no beginning or ending
but just a happy path of colors and sounds
until we reached its perfect silence.
It is too simple a day later
to be certain of cause and effect,
for yesterday they were mostly not,
hardly visible from one glance to another:
it just all happened—and perhaps
we have reasons to be thankful
that it was.

November 1, 2009

(for Martin Murphy)

Great jets of wind
had exiled the leaves
(a lawn I had to rake
now wonderfully cleared),
and though grim November,
the Feast of All Saints,
it was too bright and sunny
to celebrate the dead
but a day to honor birds—
the swans newly on the river,
an eagle in patriotic profile,
great flotillas of assorted ducks,
and a certain ten grams of being,
a red-breasted nuthatch.

As I refilled the bird feeders,
he took a casual perch,
oblivious and unconcerned,
bare inches away from me.
I could hear him pecking suet,
watched him move to peanuts,
and morsel firmly grasped,
he departed in a flutter,
brushing my head with a wing,
and later that night,
it was clear but nearly starless,
a full moon almost embracing
a lone planet nearby, another
of the day's sweet proximities.

The Importance of Being Unimportant

It's good to be unimportant,
to have no particular duties,
no one waiting for a decision;

and so to be a free soul,
free to watch the fall leaves
and ponder the meaning of asters;

to worry about the birds
who might have lingered
too long into the chill;

to read unimportant books
that might have mattered
in a youth, fifty years ago,

those dim and distant days
when everything seemed important.

The Transports of a Friday Night

You must forgive me if I am too happy,
reading poetry and listening to music:
Vaughan Williams dancing
through an English meadow,
Andrew Marvel walking his lady love
along the scented banks of the Ganges,
and in the St. Louis of long ago,
Stan the Man standing at the plate.
Outside my window I am sure
there is a heaven full of stars,
and these gifts are almost too much to bear,
so difficult to leave when it is time
to close the day and find sleep,
to consider the needs of tomorrow,
but I linger, banish thought,
and nudge myself into the quiet
that is eternity, and I am thankful.

What I Think I Know

I cannot be faithless to my own conviction of values.

—Alfred Kazin, Journals

I will not renounce belief
simply because there is too much of it,
or refuse to worship
because the world is full of idols.

There's no honor in certainties
that displace reflection,
nor any shame in doubts
before the span of our choices.

Dear God, let us be true
to what we think we know,
manage each day for itself,
let eternity be what it will,

pray for knowledge instead of judgment,
give thanks for every waking.

Thinking about Love

Someone sang of love, sweet love,
and it's clear what was meant:
surely those early ventures,

those remote bits of eternity,
when eyes and skin were alight
with the presence, the holy proximity

of the beloved, in all those places:
the dreary apartment, a faraway beach,
the long train ride across the city;

those times when the sky itself
seemed so unimportant
compared to the blood in its surge,

all so long ago and so distant
from the quiet of this evening.

A Farewell

If suddenly it were the end of the world,
what difference would it make?
The void does not speak,

and beyond my very self,
the leaves still dance in the breeze,
a motion of life on Sunday morning,

and the sun still shines.
People are still there, some shopping,
and some, a miracle, are singing.

The newspaper might or might not come;
the dog must stop to sniff
and expects her dinner at four;

and whatever I did or did not,
to the end, I kept on loving you.

A Reply

Remember what we did today, darling. Looks like I've got you just where I want you and know that I'm just where I want to be. I love you so very much, you know, for today, tomorrow and always.

—Your almost-wife
(April 8, 1967)

Forty years later it's a mystery:
I cannot tell you what we did
one early spring day in Chicago.
Memory is a poor vessel,
if vessel at all. Feelings abound,
but facts are no more,
precious immediacy lost.

So let the years have their sway;
let every detail, soft or sharp,
be ephemeral except ourselves,
what we do for one another.

As for the rest,
forty years will do for always.
I am still in the same place
and hope you are, too,
my eternal wife.

A World in Round

It's a world quite round,
the great globe itself,
encircled by its equator;

in its sky, a sun and a moon,
the dots of stars and planets
across the arc of a winter night;

and then smaller, in a summer garden,
the warm and glowing orbs
of cosmos, zinnias, and sunflowers;

and still closer, our eyes
fixed on each other,
our four hands joined

to make the circle of our being:
neither you nor I but we two.

Christmas Eve 2014

It could be lonely in this room
as I sit by myself at ten o'clock,
but it isn't. Not at all,
for I am surrounded by people,
the voices of souls I once knew,
the silence of those I did not;
by parents and ancestors,
people I did not know well enough,
and the questions I never asked them.

There are cousins and friends,
the people I watch through the distance
but still know, no matter the miles,
and those I saw a few hours ago:
my neighbor, whose husband is dying,
and children whose energy
almost frightens these old bones;
and even more, all the people unmet,
those who will teach me things
I will wish I had known ages ago;

and then a wife of forty-seven years,
who slumbers in the next room,
confident that I will soon join her.

A Long Marriage

Forgive me if I have forgotten
our children in their infancy
and years of their schooling,
but I have not forgotten
the days when they were born,
nor will I ever forget
when you and I first met,
nor that night when our flesh
began to meld into a whole.
Forgive me if I do not recall
the early struggles of each day,
duties of together unequally shared,
but this alliance has survived
over decades we can barely count;
and forgive me if I have forgotten
last Tuesday, even yesterday morning,
or what we discussed at lunch,
but I still remember one evening
when we said things to each other
and dared that all this would last.

Chicago

As we arrived from Dixie in 1951,
a walk in the Loop and lunch at the Berghof
were only the first act in the show.
There were huge buildings and miles of train yards,
the museums and Marshall Field's,
the zoo, the El, and the aquarium,
and on the South Side, the White Sox.

In the city, alien worlds sat side by side.
The bums outside Pacific Garden Mission
were shambling just two narrow blocks
from the luxury of Michigan Avenue,
and a few lanes of traffic and Comiskey Park
separated Irish Bridgeport and the mayor
from the sullen towers of the Taylor Homes.

The movie theaters were a marvel,
where the shows began at 9:00 a.m.;
there were diners that never closed,
newsstands with papers in unknown languages,
magazines with anatomy lessons,
and the happy chaos of New Year's Eve
at the corner of State and Randolph.

Long ago, in pursuit of true love,
I memorized twenty miles of subway stations
and pledged my eternal devotion to her
outside the doors of Symphony Hall
with a penny ring bought on Wabash Avenue.
Sadly enough, the Berghof is no more,
and I am long gone to other places,
but when I am back, I still hear all the songs.

Moments, a Little Later

Across the years, the moments matter:
that glimpse along the roadside
of the ironweed or the New England aster,
those brilliant purples holding forth
against the dun of autumn grasses;
that smile from someone we love
or someone we do not know at all,
when some word or gesture was perfect;
or on tonight's stroll along the houses
as we saw the lights in the windows
standing in for human love,
and above, on this chilly evening,
the stars visible in their great bowl
posed above this place where we live;
and though these are only moments,
they contain our eternity,
and for the rest of our lives,
we will be waiting for the next moments.

Snowfall at Night

I hear the air alive with snow,
a music in the winter night.
The ground reflects a spectral glow
against the trees redrawn in white.

The flakes are notes to make a theme,
a sound of snow to bury doubt,
the stolid whiteness and the dream
of calm within and peace without.

Full Moon

In winter, moon and snow make light,
a piece of day within the night.

It almost seems beneath the glow,
there's something rare that has to grow,

as if some fire from down below
were rising just to kindle snow,

and doing so, lit up belief
and moved my eyes away from grief.

Sunday at Bever Park

Sunday afternoon at the park,
the dog was happy with her scents,
and I, listening to warblers,

thought about the beauty of sound
and sight too: women far too young
to be the mothers of their children.

So far have I progressed,
accumulated so many days,
that everything beyond myself

seems incomparably young,
but what a pleasure it is
to think that days have no conclusion,

that the end of my chapter
is neither the end of spring anemones
nor of mothers and children.

Today

Now is the time that we have:
tomorrow is a thought,
which may or may not be;
thus, now is the time
to listen to that bluebird
on a roof across the street,
to sing with the song sparrow
who graces the world
from behind your house,
to watch your favorite dog
alive with spring scents
as the snow surely melts,
to love the light of March
and forget the dark of January;
to find the ones you love
and tell them that it is so;
to think about God
and to give thanks,
for without this now,
there is nothing.

The Scarlet Tanager

So often our shy visitor,
heard but rarely seen,
he's been at our bird bath
three days running now,
a near miracle.

You haven't seen red
until you've spied this fellow,
a dapper Latin gent
who graces northern summer
with flaming crimson;

and brilliant is only a fraction
of what could be said
about a color
nearly inconceivable in a place
that knows winter.

Cancer

(for J. Y. S. and J. L. B.)

There it is, the unspeakable word:
that body where we have lived
through so many good years
has decided to betray us,
sending cells with death for purpose;
and all that lovely skin,
those organs that sustained us,
the blood that pulsed
and made us feel alive
can no longer be trusted.
There are no assurances:
the wisdom of our times contains
only the comfort of probabilities,
and so we pray that what it knows
is a sufficient enemy;
but mostly we must trust ourselves,
our thoughts, and what we believe
to bring us to some suitable end,
whether tomorrow or years to come,
the place where we belong
and where we know
that we have done all we can.

The Asters

Today I've been pondering
choice, a slippery matter,
and all the asters
in their great variety:

New England and arrow-leafed,
azure, heath and willow,
and some I cannot parse,
which remain merely asters.

They are the last before the dark
and the most patient of souls,
waiting the entire summer
before coming into flower

and, without the weight of choice,
bloom, because they must.

The Tree Outside That Window

Those leaves I have watched for weeks,
my link to the rhythms that govern,
are at last yellowing and about to drop;
and instead of mourning the loss,

I think of notes of music,
which fade, one by one, once heard,
and thus no tune is ever the same,
no matter how often played;

and likewise that tree, too, which passes
through the leaves of summer and those of fall,
is never the same from one Sunday to the next.
But no song is lost; the tree is resolute,

and for our waiting, next season
the leaves will quaver more gracefully:
a sharper drama, a clearer melody,
an ever-brighter green.

For Leo Michael

(before he was born)

The news of your being
has stirred us to imaginings.
We know we have seen you,
have perhaps touched your hand,

and because you will give us yourself,
we must make ready the world
where you will be moving,
the countless rooms and fields

that you will fill with moments:
if only there were time
and means enough
to make them perfect!

Still, be brave, little swimmer,
and come to join us.

The Moth

Hands tightly joined,
we were making our way
down the hall stairs
that joined apartment 2B
to the wider world
when he spied it lying still,
the dead moth on a step,
a dry and stiff-winged husk,
and offered his assessment,
"Nigh, nigh, buggy."
This became the refrain
of our comings and goings.

Night, night, indeed!
Buggy, you are no more,
and how am I to concoct
the fact of your nothing
for this small person,
let alone a valedictory
for a sparrow or his cat?
Such thinking is not easy.

Then a few days later,
the moth was gone,
tidied into its forever,
and we talked of other things.

For Maya Grace

(before she was born)

We can see you as clearly
as we know your name,
your smiles and steps
now joined to each day.

We find you in the midst
of fields and flowers,
imagine conversations
about birds and moons,
and, holding your hand,
set off to find them.

Sweet girl, your place is here,
and as we wait for you
to cross the great divide,
our arms and our hearts are open.

The Moth, Revisited

Today it's no longer about the moth,
and you are no longer that small boy
stretching for a few words
but grown into ideas and sentences.

First it was a dead sparrow,
fallen at the edge of the woods,
that you found earlier this autumn
and presented to your mother;

and now a trip to the vet
with a cat who was failing,
an awful ride back home,
an empty carrier to take in;

and so you have met it,
touched the cold clay,
too soon witnessed the void
so difficult to reconcile;

and though words should dance
to make the day lighter,
sometimes thoughts are heavy
and cannot lift their feet.

The Streams of Pennsylvania

Can any marvel equal water?
Even a mere drainage ditch
bubbling with spring runoff
is magic to small children,

who toss in stick after stick
(boats of great dimension)
and measure their progress
as they float down the hillside;

eagerly crouching at the culverts,
watching the fleet's progress
from entrance through exit
and on to new passages;

all ending at the bottom of the road,
water pouring into a nameless stream
flowing in unknown ways,
but surely on to the Susquehanna

and finally reaching the Chesapeake,
that great expanse of water—
the perfect mystery of ocean
on a perfect spring day.

The Quick and the Dead

Who peoples my world?
At my age it is not a simple question,
as time pulls me between two domains:
the dead, where I roam through memories,
afternoons from decades ago,
though in my mind, still as green
as the leaves on summer trees.
I see the people I left behind,
their faces and even scents still as fresh
as they were on some actual day,
real and surely not imagined,
but somehow all is silence;
so I must turn to the living,
to children who know no restraint,
to the voices of those I love,
whether smooth or strident,
for the joy of sounds, and even noise,
and, yes—suffer the rough edges
of life as it will be carried out,
all the dear unplanned days
where one foot follows the next
in a nearly endless progress,
and with a great burden of gratitude,
I move toward the places I must find.

Waiting for Maya

Hearing that she might arrive in advance
of the day determined by the exact sciences,
we set off in a rush through five states,
arriving only to continue waiting
as the goddess of delivery was in no hurry,
and the one person who might know
was in no position to tell us about it.

In the warm days of late summer,
we learned the way to the hospital,
had lemonade and popcorn at the fair,
checked and rechecked the baby's want list,
killing time on mundane chores
while a fretting daughter was unsoothed
by a doctor who told her not to worry.

The brother-to-be, an old hand with grandparents,
charmed us with new learning and language.
At age three he has new interests
in the laws of cause and effect,
generating endless streams of questions,
turning back each answer with "why?"
and asking each day if the baby would come.

Still content with her watery confines,
she refused to emerge from hiding,
and the days became a week;
but then the sudden midnight alarm,
and after a few hours she was here,
bringing her brightness to the world,
and we all felt that ancient shiver
as a new love stepped in beside us.

A Place to Be

There is no better place,
not even Camelot or Byzantium.
You step outside your door,

and looking through the trees,
that great curtain of leaves,
are the sky, the sun, the clouds—

everything you could imagine—
the green, blue, and white
in their great curves:

the birds in their flights
underneath a happy sun
and, later, stars dotting the dark.

That's where you might want to go,
but feet must remain
where gravity rules them,

but not thoughts—
which can soar in these words
as high as any swallow.

The Lovers

I saw them walking along the street,
a man and woman, a couple
(to my eyes impossibly young),
as handsome as this spring day.

Smiling, their fingers entwined,
they were off to some destination,
and though I could worry these two
into the weight of love's long years,

the pain and glory of shared devotion,
let it not be so today:
let them love for an afternoon
as if it were an eternity,

play the note of each today
before tomorrow tears it apart.

The Snake

I startled a snake
gliding through the rocks
near the corner of the house—
or did the snake startle me?

Each of us froze in his spot,
locked in place for a long moment,
and then he moved,
as only a serpent can,

a symmetry of undulations,
sliding into a narrow hole.
There would be no discussions
with this shining fellow,

no commerce between our races,
only this silent meeting,
and then that long separation
we have known since Eden.

A Blessing

He has never seen God/but once or twice he believes/he has
heard him.
                                        —*a haiku by W.H. Auden*

I've never been summoned
to perform a task like Abraham
or sentenced to the miseries of Job.

Far from it: it's all been ordinary—
the flat tires and the shopping,
washing windows and paying the bills;

the reprieve of easy temptations
and most hints of tragedy
soon balanced by some gift.

Yet even a modest life
must find some reference
to what is always true,

to wonder and gratitude,
some whisper of a voice.

July 25, 2011

Is it a world to find or to make?
What we see on a day in July
or how we chance to see it?

Surrounded by lavender bergamot,
the coneflowers' gold,
and the blue stars of bellflower,

I might lean to discovery:
no way my thoughts alone
could draw all this bright beauty,

but think also of the need
to find names for such happiness—
and must give the dream its due.

The End of Summer

There's a note from the katydids,
loud and clear in mid-August,
and from the yellow primrose
whose blooms wait all summer,
now clustered along the road.
It's the sad innocence of summer,
when nature grows beyond measure,
fast and slow, both early and late,
with no concern for the weather,
as if sun and warm rain were forever.
But we know loss before it happens—
memories of parents alive but failing,
of fragile loves and a passing friend,
those faces sure to disappear:
the sadness coded in our very bones,
though autumn is still weeks away.

Worlds

The world you see
may not be the world you know,
but it hardly matters.

It's likely not the world
that really is, either:
that magic, unmeaning web,

its systems of blood and protein,
of atoms and quarks,
of nothing quite as palpable

as children running into your arms,
undulating goldfinches above,
or the dusty asters of October;

and perhaps the world is simply
the one you do not forget,
the one you find words for.

October 13

The afternoon had that feeling,
the words of a good-bye,
a day to count as the last.

The park was full of people,
alive with children and dogs,
and the last sunbathers,

drowning in the warmth
of a sun already moving south,
near the end of its rule;

and for those two lovers,
a last day to hold hands,
eyes fixed, across a picnic table;

and who could question love
on any day, let alone this one,
this last day to be a careless soul?

A Poem for My Latest Birthday

Having reached my eighth decade,
I have no choice but happiness:
I've moved many days further along
than most of my ancestors,
even most of the people
who have lived on this earth,
and though I have been leisurely
in finding grace, it still comes.

After days of rain and dank,
the stars once more dot the skies,
those great enemies of gloom,
dear signals of our eternal
that counter the dark,
reminding me I know descendants,
people to carry goodness forward,
who'll remember that I loved
the birds, the flowers, and them;
and with these blessings
and others, more than I can count,
I am ready for peace,
a place where something seems right,
if only for tonight, or always.

All Saints' Day 2015

(for Joanne White)

I was listening to a sermon on gratitude,
one of my favorite subjects,
and outside the window
my favorite tree, still mostly green,
its leaves fluttering in the breeze,
surrounded by the skeletal branches
of its neighboring trees,
was in a last dance to the summer,
a witness to all that had grown
before winter made it a memory,
and above the tree, smoky clouds
rolled over the distant Tussey range.
I gave thanks for this world,
which gives us everything we need,
both great beauty and breakfast,
and all those great souls,
both the saints and the parents,
who have made us what we are;
and then, at the conclusion
of our meeting with the holy mysteries,
I reported for duty at the kitchen sink,
ready for spoons and coffee cups
and eternally grateful
to have some useful work to do,
to put paid to that evil myth
that we are somehow self-sufficient,
for at the end of any day,
someone must do the dishes.

An Ordinary Night in Boalsburg, Pennsylvania

Walking under the stars,
my thoughts are brought to earth
by the odors of a skunk,
some creature doing its work,
pursuing the aims of life,
and I feel somehow settled.
My dog is leading the way,
and we are going somewhere
that only she knows how to find.

It is brighter to the east,
where there are no streetlights,
and I can see Orion once more,
now lifting his great belt
as November moves toward winter,
and we arrive at no place very special,
except, perhaps, that there are scents,
knowledge I cannot share with Maisie,
but I am happy to be with my friend
on some great voyage of discovery;
and unlike that of old Balboa
standing on his peak in Darien,
this one, sooner or later,
will bring us back home.

November 22, 2013

It's a day full of memories,
of English 201 fifty years ago,
where I learned the news,
but today is not for old business
as my dog and I walk
our usual path along the river,

she with her vocation of smells,
while I look for cormorants,
those great brown fellows
still here a few days ago,
birds that pose like Draculas,
their wings spread out to dry,

who now seem to have departed,
to have given up on the summer,
and high time on this cold day,
for despite blue to the horizons
and a bright, golden sun,
no one can deny what must be.

Life Continues

That old Greek had it right,
the one who wrote about streams,
and how—no matter where we step—
the stream is ever changing
as the water keeps rolling on.
Days do move along to heartbeats
in a great stew of events and feelings,
never coming to any sort of end,
which leaves me baffled
by all the careless talk of closure,
that we could stay the moment
and, at will, arrive at conclusions.
Such magic can only be granted
to a singular genius, a Vermeer
capturing the girl with her balance,
life in a veritable equipoise,
an illusion that time no longer is
as we look at her beauty,
stopped in its moment;
or perhaps, more grimly,
we might wander into that event,
the one that awaits us all,
but that we will never know,
the one leaving these lines unsaid;
and so I am happy to be somewhere,
in a place to give thanks
for this bright and halting process,
for Vermeer, and for these lines.

Destinations

I've learned to walk a crooked line,
to find my way by going there,
and look for maps but find a prayer,
the compass that my feet define.

Uncertainty is not malign
if I can size each step with care.
I've learned to walk a crooked line,
to find my way by going there.

Perfection is a pointless shrine.
How well I know not to despair
that every day requires repair.
Whatever comes, I make it mine:
I've learned to walk a crooked line.

Made in the
USA
Columbia, SC